I0424434

Rebuilding
The
Democratic Party
From The Grassroots

Rebuilding
The
Democratic Party
From The Grassroots

◆

The Ultimate Guidebook For Democrats

Drucilla Badurina and
Shawn M. O'Donnell

iUniverse, Inc.
New York Lincoln Shanghai

Rebuilding The Democratic Party From The Grassroots
The Ultimate Guidebook For Democrats

Copyright © 2005 by Drucilla Badurina and Shawn M. O'Donnell

All rights reserved. No part of this book may be used or reproduced by any means, graphic, electronic, or mechanical, including photocopying, recording, taping or by any information storage retrieval system without the written permission of the publisher except in the case of brief quotations embodied in critical articles and reviews.

iUniverse books may be ordered through booksellers or by contacting:

iUniverse
2021 Pine Lake Road, Suite 100
Lincoln, NE 68512
www.iuniverse.com
1-800-Authors (1-800-288-4677)

Copies of this book may be purchased in bulk by special arrangement with the publisher.

ISBN-13: 978-0-595-35620-1 (pbk)
ISBN-13: 978-0-595-80099-5 (ebk)
ISBN-10: 0-595-35620-6 (pbk)
ISBN-10: 0-595-80099-8 (ebk)

Printed in the United States of America

To all those great Democrats who have gone before us including:
Kazimir Anton Badurina
Barbara Malnar Badurina
Joseph Eugene O'Donnell
Paul Vincent Varga

Contents

Preface

After losing another race for the White House, as well as becoming an even smaller minority in Congress, Democrats need to evaluate what went wrong in 2004 and what to do to transform defeat into future victory. There is no doubt the current Democratic Party needs to change. In order for the new shoots of plants and trees to thrive, old, dead branches need to be trimmed away.

Growing or re-growing an organization begins from the bottom up, not the top down. The Democratic Party must return to its roots, its grassroots, and rebuild itself as an old fashioned, twenty-first century party. This book provides an analysis of the 2004 election, why the Democratic Party lost, and serves as a ready guide for those who seek to take the Democratic Party back to the future, back to its values, back to the people.

PART I
How to Lose an Election Democratic Style

2004 Presidential Campaign
What National Campaign?

When John F. Kerry, the Democratic Party's candidate, lost the 2004 presidential election, over 56 million stunned Kerry voters throughout the United States asked the same questions over and over again: How could Kerry lose to George W. Bush? What happened to the outpouring of Kerry support not seen since John Fitzgerald Kennedy? Didn't they vote? How can it be almost déjà vu of 2000 all over again? Who is to blame? What happens now?

Among the explanations offered for the election debacle were: Republican dirty tricks and a smear campaign; the impact of FOX Entertainment News Channel, regarded by educated media observers as the 24/7 voice of Republican propaganda; NASCAR dads; security moms; evangelical or religious fundamentalist voters; red (Republican voting majority) states vs. blue (Democratic voting majority) states; etc.

From the beginning, the Kerry campaign controlled the choice of where and how to run. When John Kerry, his advisors, and staff chose not to run a national campaign, the "writing was on the wall."

According to the contact information provided at johnkerry.com, no Kerry campaign office existed in the states of Alabama, Alaska, Connecticut, Delaware, Georgia, Hawaii, Indiana, Iowa, Kansas, Louisiana, Mississippi, Montana, North Dakota, South Carolina, South Dakota, Tennessee, Utah, and Wyoming. A total of nineteen states did not even have an official Kerry headquarters. There was no place that was the important visible presence, a location for face to face grassroots interaction where state Democrats and other Kerry supporters could gather, strategize, work, or even physically obtain campaign materials.

Electoral College Strategy

Basic to every discussion of presidential elections is the knowledge that, currently, a citizen's vote in one state is not equivalent to a citizen's vote in another state. Under the system in use in the United States today, 538 Electoral College electors, one per senator and every representative from each state, elect the president and vice-president, usually casting their ballots for the candidate who wins the popular vote in their state. In addition, the District of Columbia has three votes. The winner of the election is the candidate who receives a majority of votes, more than 270.

In November of 2000, George W. Bush lost the popular vote for President of the United States to Albert A. Gore, Jr. Thousands of voters in Florida were disenfranchised by a decision of the U.S. Supreme Court to stop the Florida vote recount. Bush was awarded all of Florida's electoral votes and thus "won" the office because of the Electoral College system. The final tally showed Bush with 271 and Gore with 266 electors' votes.

John Kerry's 2004 campaign advisors focused on pursuing a strategy they thought would get them to the magic number of 270 Electoral College votes. Kerry's campaign chose to follow a non-Southern, limited Midwestern, and Western strategy. In essence, they convinced themselves that it was possible to win without any Southern states, with the possible exception of Florida, and only selected Midwestern and Western states. Others tried to persuade Kerry to campaign on a national basis and take no state for granted, but they did not prevail. Today we know Kerry's non-Southern, limited Midwestern, and Western strategy did not work. Kerry's total shows 252 to Bush's 286 electoral votes.

John Kerry ended up winning most of the same states Al Gore won in 2000. He added New Hampshire's four electoral votes, but lost both Iowa's seven electoral votes and New Mexico's five electoral votes.

Does the Electoral College system distort election results by dividing up the vote state by state? Some say it is an institution that has outlived its usefulness because it aggregates the popular vote in what must be considered an inherently unjust manner. For example, less populous states are assured a minimum of three electoral votes, based on two senators and one representative, no matter what the population size. After the 1990 census for instance, Alaska had a population of 551,947 with three electoral votes and California had a population of 29,839,250 with fifty-four electoral votes. Therefore, Alaska had one Electoral College vote for every 183,989 residents, while California had one electoral vote for every 552,579 residents.

The Electoral College system has allowed presidential candidates who did not win the popular vote of the American electorate to win the election anyway, frustrating the will of the majority. In 1876, Rutherford B. Hayes lost the popular vote, but won the election by one electoral vote. In 1888, Benjamin Harrison lost the popular vote to Grover Cleveland, but won the election with sixty-five more Electoral College votes than Cleveland. In 2000, Bush lost the popular vote, but "won" the Electoral College vote. All three of these Electoral College presidential winners were Republicans.

On November 2, 2004, the popular and electoral votes coincided with Bush receiving over 60,600,000 popular votes while Kerry tallied over 57,200,000 votes. However, the results do not indicate what impact the Kerry campaign's decision to forgo a real national campaign in order to focus on an Electoral College victory will have on the Democratic Party in presidential elections for years to come.

Kerry's decision left millions of Democratic voters in the "red states" without a reason to vote and, more importantly, without a candidate to rally behind, which also impacted negatively on undecided and independent voters. It's certainly not surprising that 2004 saw low voter turnout numbers in non-battleground states.

It's never
too early to
think BLUE
for 2008

Who Carried the Message?

Not to be outdone by the Kerry campaign, the Democratic National Committee (DNC), the Democratic Congressional Campaign Committee (DCCC), and the numerous state Democratic Parties failed to make sure that the party fielded candidates in all of the Congressional races. Each of the following districts failed to have a Democrat on the ballot.

State	District Number(s)	Total Congressional Districts
Alabama*	06	(1 of 7)
Arizona	03, 06	(2 of 8)
California	22, 32, 33, 41	(4 of 53)
Florida	04, 07, 09, 24, 25	(5 of 25)
Georgia*	01, 06, 07, 10	(4 of 13)
Kansas*	01	(1 of 4)
Kentucky	05	(1 of 6)
Louisiana*	04	(1 of 7)
Mississippi*	01, 03	(2 of 4)
New York	25	(1 of 29)
Pennsylvania	05, 10, 19	(3 of 19)
South Carolina*	01, 03	(2 of 6)
Tennessee*	07	(1 of 9)
Texas	03, 10, 13, 14	(4 of 31)
Vermont	01	(1 of 1) seat held by an Independent
Virginia	01, 06, 07	(3 of 11)

* Indicates a state without a formal Kerry headquarters.

Thirty-six seats nationwide were left uncontested. What was the impact on the Presidential race? Even if a Democratic Party candidate increased the average turnout by only 25,000 per district, 900,000 additional voters would have gone to the polls.

Democratic Party officials might say, "So what? Some of those were losers and we chose to pass on them to concentrate on the battleground states." However, they pointedly chose to ignore the responsibility they have as Democratic Party leaders to promulgate Democratic Party ideals, values, and principles and to breathe life into the party's platform for millions of Americans. They chose, instead, what they thought would be an easy road to victory.

When the Kerry campaign decided not to bring its message to the entire nation and the DNC, the DCCC, and the state Democratic Parties did not make sure a Democratic candidate was on the ballot in every Congressional district, they not only lost the election, they lost the opportunity to solidify their Democratic base and influence American voters.

Covering Your Back

Shortly before he was to appear at the first of three presidential debates, John Kerry sent the following message to his supporters, "The other day after a rally in Ohio, a woman asked someone from our campaign to deliver a message to me. She said, 'Senator Kerry, we've got your back.' That is certainly the feeling I have as you and hundreds of thousands of others keep pouring your hearts and souls into winning this election. That support inspires me as I prepare for tonight's debate with George W. Bush."

The 2004 election did indeed find John Kerry's back supported by ready, willing, and able volunteers. Contributing their treasure, time, and talents to a unified campaign to defeat an incumbent president, Kerry's supporters covered his back time and again. For example, grassroots organizations, progressive organizations, and Democratic bloggers led the charge against the lies and distortions being promulgated by a Republican funded attack organization, the Swift Boat Veterans for Truth, long before the Kerry campaign roused itself from a seemingly clueless apathy.

However, Kerry and his campaign's actions led many supporters to conclude that neither he nor his campaign fulfilled their obligation to cover their supporters' backs. On election night, they watched as his campaign conceded prematurely, and then, they had to remind him to honor his pledge that every vote would be counted. Ultimately John Kerry, the junior senator from Massachusetts, failed to even show up on January 6, 2005 for the joint session of Congress called to confirm the results of the Electoral College vote.

Thirty-one distinguished members of the House of Representatives, led by Barbara Tubbs Jones (D-OH), and one distinguished member of the Senate, Barbara Boxer (D-CA), rightly questioned the validity of the electoral votes of the state of Ohio. Their actions required both chambers to temporarily suspend the process to allow open floor debate on the question of the voting irregularities and possible illegalities that surfaced in Ohio.

Senator Kerry's statement read in part, "I will not be taking part in a formal protest of the Ohio Electors."

PART II
Campaign Micro Studies

National Micro Case Study
Losing the Electoral College

Given the strategies followed by the Kerry campaign in 2004, and the lack of a national effort to grow the base of the Democratic Party, it's not hard to see why only three states changed their electoral preference from 2000. Losing New Mexico and Iowa further emphasized the lack of campaign support for real grassroots efforts.

Four other "red" states did get some degree of Kerry campaign support. Arkansas, North Carolina, Virginia, and West Virginia were given some consideration by Kerry's campaign during the process. Each had a fairly substantial number of electoral votes and could have mitigated other electoral losses.

Examining the fluctuating emphasis the campaign placed on each of those states, observers could conclude the following:

Arkansas with only five electoral votes apparently got the early nod for campaigning because of former President William Jefferson Clinton. However, after Clinton was sidelined by major surgery, and some polling showed erosion in Iowa, Minnesota, and Wisconsin, the Kerry camp once again seemed to shift their focus.

North Carolina with its fifteen Electoral College votes is the home of Senator John Edwards, Kerry's hand picked running mate and vice-presidential candidate. While his inclusion on the ticket was not predicated on winning in the South, many hoped his name on the ticket would shore up support in his home state and would bring Virginia's thirteen votes and West Virginia's five votes into the Democratic column.

In the end, Arkansas, North Carolina, Virginia, and West Virginia all went red.

Arkansas	Bush	573,182	Kerry	470,230
North Carolina	Bush	1,961,116	Kerry	1,525,849
Virginia	Bush	1,716,956	Kerry	1,454,742
West Virginia	Bush	417,516	Kerry	322,276

State Micro Case Study
The Commonwealth of Virginia

Virginia's Democratic Primary

On February 10, 2004, a Democratic presidential primary was held in the Commonwealth of Virginia. Given the timing of the primary, the real question on the ballot was: Do you believe any of the other candidates can stop the Democratic Party from nominating John Kerry?

At the beginning of the year, the Democratic Party's consensus front-runner was Howard Dean. It was the media who gave Dean that title, but that was because he also led most state polls, had a growing grassroots organization, innovative Internet fundraising, other money sources, and momentum. His defeat in the January caucuses in Iowa and the primary in New Hampshire defined the race by identifying a different front-runner, someone who was broadly accepted among establishment Democrats, Massachusetts senator, John F. Kerry.

Iowa and New Hampshire primary results are always assigned great importance and, in the 2004 race, it was especially so. Conventional wisdom considers the winner of the Iowa and New Hampshire primaries the odds on favorite to become the party nominee. It's taken for granted that Democrats don't like to think they are wasting their money or their votes on a losing effort. They want to go with a winner. Iowa and New Hampshire have historically helped identify that person for the party. But, in today's national picture, Virginia is almost as big and may even be more critical to the future of the Democratic Party. Virginia shows whether a Democratic candidate can compete in the South.

In 2004, some 396,233 Virginia voters essentially determined the fate of the Democratic presidential campaigns of John Edwards, Wesley Clark, and Howard Dean. Each needed a victory and each came away without one.

After entering the race too late by most standards, Wesley Clark campaigned with a southern states strategy. While he won a narrow victory in Oklahoma, he received only 36,572 votes from Virginia Democrats. Howard Dean supporters were only able to bring 27,637 voters to the polls, not nearly enough support to realistically hope to take on Kerry.

John Edwards may still be the face of the future for many in the Democratic Party, but backing from 105,504 Virginia Democrats was not enough. John Kerry ended the day with 204,142 votes. However, there was speculation that if Edwards and Kerry were the only names on the primary ballot, John Edwards would have carried the Commonwealth.

John Kerry's win in Virginia is said to have sent the message that Democrats were ready to unite around a single candidate as the best course to defeat Bush, the incumbent Republican. Most Virginians who supported Kerry were, in fact, in the Anybody But Bush (ABB) category. Many of those who voted for Kerry agreed that a Massachusetts senator would not appeal to voters in the South.

However, in commenting on his primary victory, Kerry told supporters in Virginia that Americans were voting for change, even in the South, which indicated that love of country was more important than regional differences. Considering the result of the general election, he may have been wrong.

Exit polls conducted in Virginia showed Kerry winning what many consider crucial Democratic Party core demographic groups: 55 percent of women voters, 64 percent of black voters, and 62 percent of voters over sixty-five. What they did not show was that if Kerry expected to carry his qualified "Southern Democrats" support into the general election, he would need to do a lot more work.

The great seal of the Commonwealth of Virginia contains the Latin motto "Sic Semper Tyrannis"—"Thus Always to Tyrants". The two figures are acting out the meaning of the motto. Both are warriors and it is the woman, Virtue, who is the victor over Tyranny.

Virginia's General Election
Or
Coattails Run Both Ways

For a short time during the general election campaign, the Commonwealth of Virginia was considered a battleground state and a lot of information was collected to show the Kerry campaign how to compete and win the state. Using the reverse coattail effect, Kerry could win Virginia.

If that had happened, it would have been the first time in 40 years that a Democratic presidential candidate won in Virginia. Instead, Kerry was soundly defeated garnering 45.48% of the vote to Bush's 53.68%.

The coordinated campaign concept for turning this red state to blue should have been doable. It was up to the Kerry campaign, the Democratic National Committee, the Democratic Congressional Campaign Committee, the Virginia Democratic Party, local Democratic Committees, endorsed Democratic candidates, and volunteers to carry the campaign throughout the Commonwealth. But the Democratic Party failed to even run candidates in three Congressional Districts: First, Sixth, and Seventh.

While other Congressional Districts in the State delivered as much as 66.24% of their votes for Kerry, those districts without a Democratic candidate did not even manage 40%. Check out these results:

District	Kerry	%
1	122,771	39.17
6	100,561	35.84
7	128,166	38.31

Kerry's state total ended up being 45.48%. After adjusting for these three districts, the results are markedly different and show an average of 48.75%. That adjustment is shown as follows:

District	Kerry	%
1	152,804	48.75
6	136,781	48.75
7	163,111	48.75

The result of the loss in these three districts on the outcome of the presidential race was a swing of 101,198 votes. How does that translate into the overall results? It dramatically changes the outcome of the election. Bush still carries Virginia, as evidenced by using the 48.75% number, but only by 59,821 votes.

Using another method of analyzing the results, the outcome was even closer and shows the true reverse coattail effect. If competitive Democratic candidates had run in all three districts and won only one of the three seats, Kerry's actual votes in the three districts would have increased by 131,767. Although the margin would have been slim, Bush would have gone down to defeat in Virginia. The final total would have been Kerry with 1,586,509 and Bush with 1,585,283.

However, the First, Sixth, and Seventh Congressional Districts did not run candidates and four other Virginia Congressional districts' candidates got precious little support from the Kerry campaign, the Democratic National Committee, the Democratic Congressional Campaign Committee, and the Democratic Party of Virginia.

Of special note: David Ashe in the Second Congressional District, Al Weed in the Fifth, and Ken Longmyer in the Eleventh ran credible campaigns. In the end, they each lacked the financial resources and Democratic Party support necessary to compete against well organized and well funded Republican Congressional campaigns.

Also noteworthy was the well-organized campaign of Third Congressional District Congressman, incumbent Robert C. "Bobby" Scott. He not only crushed his Republican opponent 70% to 30%, but his coordinated campaign to help John Kerry resulted in Kerry receiving almost as many votes as Scott. Final tallies show Kerry with 158,561 votes to Bush's 79,302 while Scott received 159,373 votes versus his Republican opponent's 70,194.

Kerry campaign officials in Virginia point out that over $2,000,000 with up to thirty-four paid staffers set a precedent in Virginia Democratic Party presidential politics.

While that type of spending may seem significant to some, in Virginia's Eleventh Congressional District race, Tom Davis, the Republican incumbent, reported contributions of $2,147,960 against Ken Longmyer, the Democratic challenger, who reported contributions of only $74,796. Vote totals for the eleventh show Davis with 186,299 and Longmyer with 118,305. Those numbers translate to $11.53 per vote for Davis and $0.63 per vote for Longmyer.

The 2003-2004 election cycle reports filed with the Federal Election Commission show Republicans receiving contributions of $14,917,912 while contributions to Democrats totaled only $6,518,861.

What is clear from the analysis is that for John Kerry, a Massachusetts senator, to have won voters in Virginia and elsewhere in the South, he needed Democratic candidates in every race to help pull him up.

Local Micro Case Study
Fredericksburg, Virginia

One way to review and analyze the 2004 Presidential election is to scrutinize a specific locality. This is a micro case study—an examination and analysis—of why John Kerry and John Edwards lost this election. Virginia's First Congressional District was one of three Virginia Congressional Districts (the other two, the Sixth and Seventh) that did not run any Democratic candidate for a seat in the U. S. House of Representatives against incumbent Republicans in the 2004 election. This was a repeat of the 2002 Congressional elections when the First Congressional District also failed to have a Democratic challenger on the ballot.

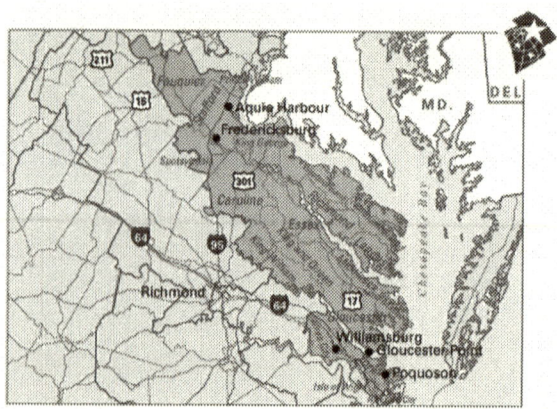

On the northern end of Virginia's First Congressional District are three contiguous counties/city: Stafford County, the city of Fredericksburg, and Spotsylvania County, each with a Democratic Committee. (The First Congressional District consists of the following: Essex, Gloucester, King and Queen, King William, Lancaster, Mathews, Middlesex, Northumberland, Richmond, Stafford, Westmoreland and York Counties; the Cities of Fredericksburg, Poquoson and Williamsburg; part of Caroline County; part of Fauquier County; part of James

City County; part of Prince William County; part of Spotsylvania County; part of the City of Hampton; and part of the City of Newport News.)

While all three counties appear in this analysis, the primary focus will be on the Fredericksburg Democratic Committee (FDC) and its role as an official Democratic Party entity in the 2004 presidential campaign and election.

The Stafford, Spotsylvania, and Fredericksburg Democratic Party Committees are formally called the Stafford Democratic Committee, the Spotsylvania Democratic Committee, and the Fredericksburg Democratic Committee. Throughout this analysis, for brevity, Fredericksburg will be referred to as the FDC, Stafford the STDC, and Spotsylvania the SPDC.

Dancing in the Dark
Post Democratic Primary

On June 9, two months after Kerry won the Virginia Democratic primary, an outdoor fundraiser with a Polynesian theme was held by the STDC, proceeds of which went to the committee and Get Out the Vote (GOTV). Guest speakers were Virginia Democratic state office holders. Entertainment was provided by an amateur group of Polynesian dancers. Kerry campaign materials were available but not really promoted. Attendees at the event seemed to be the area's established Democratic Party cliques, well known to each other, representing Stafford, Fredericksburg, and Spotsylvania.

The FDC chairperson was asked by some of the few newcomers present at the fundraiser, who were interested in becoming involved in the upcoming presidential election, when the next meeting of the FDC would be held. They were told that meetings occurred on the first Saturday of every month, but there would be none in July since that was the Fourth of July weekend.

Later discoveries:

1. These were informal, coffee klatch gatherings, not formal meetings, of the regional tri-county Democratic Committees of Stafford, Fredericksburg, and Spotsylvania.

2. There had been no formal meeting of the FDC for a long time.

3. Even though this was an important presidential election, it did not seem to warrant scheduling extra meetings in those few short months prior to the election despite increasing numbers of people wishing to volunteer and/or "do something" during this election.

The Fredericksburg chair also was asked by the newcomers why the First Congressional District had no Democratic candidate challenging the Republican incumbent, Jo Ann Davis. The answer given by the chairperson was that a potential candidate had "backed out at the last minute."

Later discoveries:

1. This was one of many ever-changing reasons for not fielding a Democratic Congressional candidate.

2. The potential candidate had withdrawn by October of 2003, leaving plenty of time to run another candidate.

3. The chairperson of the FDC was also the chair of the First Congressional District Committee.

4. The failed history of the First Congressional District shows no Democratic Party candidate in the recent elections of 2002, 1998, and 1996.

At that fundraiser, the amateur entertainment proved to be a foreshadowing of the reality of the Democratic Party in the area. By the time the speakers had finished, it was almost completely dark. Explanations of the dances by the head of the troupe were practically inaudible because there was no microphone. Shortly after the dance leader plugged in the boom box that provided the music, it blew a fuse and the few lights, which barely illuminated the dancers, went out. The dancers stood around and/or danced in the dark, where most of the audience could not see them. Bottom line: there was an obvious lack of planning including no contingency planning, since committee people were running around clueless. Newcomers left the fundraiser dismayed by their first encounter with the area's Democratic Party.

Later discoveries:

1. Newcomers[1] to Fredericksburg who had been active Democrats in their former locales and wanted to become active again in their new city found their attempts less than welcome.

---

1. *In many localities, particularly in the South, persons who have moved from elsewhere, usually the North, yet have resided in a town for a quarter of a century or more are still thought of as newcomers or "come here's" by local society.*

2. Many newcomers who called the FDC number listed in the phone book and left contact messages usually never had their calls returned.

3. The FDC had no web site and/or contact email address.

4. A search on the Internet for the FDC led to the STDC site and the monthly informal, regional, tri-county Democratic Party coffee klatch.

5. Many newcomers who attended a monthly regional session never returned, frustrated by the disorganization, lack of leadership, and lack of any effective activities.

Countdown to Election: 90 Days

August 2004
Who's in Charge?

Neither the FDC nor the Kerry campaign had any local headquarters, not even a temporary storefront, set up during this important presidential election. There was no Democratic Party or candidate campaign visibility in the area. Because there was no effective presence in Fredericksburg, either by the Democratic Party or the Kerry campaign, individual volunteers' efforts had to fill the gaping hole.

For example, the authors of this analysis, who had taken a 90 day hiatus through Election Day to volunteer for the national Kerry campaign, traveled to Kerry headquarters in Washington, D.C. the day after the convention ended. Nothing was ready to go there, just a skeleton crew with little information.

Unfortunately, throughout the campaign, the Kerry headquarters in Washington, D.C. was not user friendly. The offices were on the 19th floor of a downtown building where one had to pass the approval of an armed guard in the lobby.

The offices themselves were not very well signed for easy identification and a receptionist dressed in cut-off jeans and T-shirt somehow didn't create the best image. Moreover, the staff members were not able to answer many basic questions and didn't know how to handle certain situations. For instance, they did not know how to handle in person donations, whether by cash, check or credit card. Some average Kerry supporters are not credit card devotees—checks and cash only—and, since no campaign staffer/volunteer knew how to deal with it, these potential cash/check donors left, unable to donate because of lack of contingency planning for checks and cash.

This was later a problem on many Democratic candidates' individual web sites. There was no information on how to make a donation via check and postal mail. It was a potential donation loss because many people using the Internet don't use credit cards for a variety of reasons.

The authors were directed to a supplier's warehouse in the city where they purchased large quantities of Kerry campaign gear and materials for personal use and free distribution. Throughout September and October, they continued to make trips to Washington, D.C. and Richmond, which by then began stocking product, for campaign materials such as yard signs and bumper stickers, etc.

Since the FDC and Kerry campaign were doing nothing that was visible or effective, the authors and later other interested individuals became suppliers of campaign materials, and their cars and houses turned into distribution centers. Their yards, houses, cars, and persons were festooned with Kerry gear and materials. These people, not the FDC or the "official" Kerry campaign, spearheaded the "show the flag" visibility campaign in early August and continued throughout September, October, and November.

Also in August, one of the authors began an informal poll. From the end of the Democratic convention, five days a week, through October 31, wearing Kerry gear (T-shirt, cap, etc.) one of the authors took five mile walks through the city's streets using varying routes. Reaction to the Kerry gear from Kerry supporters (thumbs up, cheering, asking for Kerry materials, etc.) or Bush supporters (middle finger up, jeering, cursing, mumbling, etc.) provided data for a bellwether poll. Daily and weekly results of this informal poll told the authors, long before any official word, that Virginia should be a battleground state.

Immediately after the Democratic convention, the authors officially joined the Kerry national campaign as members of the Media Corps, Internet Team, and National Ethnic Outreach with special emphasis on outreach to small and mid-size business owners, Roman Catholics, and specific ethnic groups. One of the authors was 187 in output among over 1,000,000 volunteers nationwide, while the other was in the top 1,000.

Countdown to Election: 60 Days

September 2004

With the election less than two months away, at the monthly regional coffee klatch, the FDC chair's primary topic was the experience of attending the Democratic National Convention as a delegate. There was no discussion or explanation by the chair about organized campaign preparations, not even the necessary basics. There was no well designed and effectually implemented canvassing plan presented. Canvassing should have begun immediately after the primary and been completed before the convention or at least before the end of August to identify Democratic voters and other Kerry supporters in Fredericksburg.

The chair and other officials of the FDC were just beginning conversations (a free-for-all-everyone-talking-at-once exercise) at the gathering about where and how to obtain Kerry campaign materials! It was apparent that no strategic planning had been done or seemed to be in the works. It was as if a presidential election every four years was a surprise.

At this regional Democratic Party, first-Saturday-of-the-month coffee klatch, which the FDC chair erroneously led newcomers to believe was the city's Democratic Party's regular, official meeting, the usual attendance sheet was passed around, on which attendees filled in contact information that was collected by the chair.

However, even after providing this information every month, newcomers from Fredericksburg were never contacted by the city's Democratic Party about any GOTV efforts, special campaign meetings, or special election information. They received no emails, phone calls, postcards, nothing. It seemed to be a monthly mystery sign in, perhaps for a raffle at the December meeting, who knows? It certainly didn't seem to be utilized for any effective campaign effort during this presidential election year.

While the FDC was still trying to find Kerry campaign and Democratic Party materials in time for the next meeting in October, less than four weeks before the election, the area was blossoming with signs, many of which were obtained from the authors who also organized, worked and/or hosted the following events during September:

Show the Flag for Kerry: A walking tour of their hometown on Labor Day by Kerry supporters wearing campaign gear and insignia.

Voter Registration at the local VRE/Amtrak train station: Met afternoon and evening trains to distribute voter registration forms.

College Night: (authors' house) A town and gown meet and greet for information and campaign idea sharing between local college and town Democrats. Unfortunately, none of the college Democrats seemed interested enough in the campaign or election to attend while many Democratic town newcomers were.

First Debate Party: (authors' house) An energized gathering for the first presidential debate. According to the official Kerry event site, this was the only formally scheduled debate party within the Fredericksburg Democratic Party's boundaries.

Local Civic Association Block Party: Organized and manned a voter registration/absentee ballot information/forms table and a Kerry materials distribution table with campaign items like yard signs and bumper stickers that the authors had purchased to give away.

The authors attended the Virginia Victory '04 Democratic Volunteer Organizing Convention in Richmond, Virginia during the middle of September. They were the only attendees from Fredericksburg, Stafford county, and Spotsylvania county.

Countdown to Election: 30 Days

October 2004

At this monthly, Democratic Party, regional coffee klatch, campaign material acquisition still hadn't been satisfactorily solved. It seemed that the FDC chair's main concern was that there must be adequate numbers of campaign signs at the polling places. Four weeks before the election when campaign signs should have been distributed by the FDC and been sprouting from every Kerry supporter's yard, the chair instead was concerned about keeping enough signs for the polling places where they were least needed.

Also, there had been no canvassing done to identify Kerry supporters/voters. There still was no discussion or resolution led by the chair at the October meeting for any canvassing for Democratic and Kerry voter identification. The most basic requirement of any Democratic Party campaign wasn't even on the radar scope of the FDC. The paid Kerry area representative, also an FDC member, did announce plans for a phone bank.

Four weeks before the election, and there were very few campaign materials available at October's, regional Democratic coffee klatch. It was a replay of September's breakfast get together. The chair and other officials neither offered nor explained any strategic or tactical plans for the campaign to the attendees. Thirty-one days before the election and only amorphous, disorganized ideas were floating around. Again, it was apparent that a presidential election occurring every four years seemed unexpected. After the meeting, the chair began selling the few available bumper stickers at varying prices, even though they were obtainable elsewhere for free!

Later that month, about two weeks before the election, at the request of the FDC chair, a helper contacted a Kerry volunteer to ask for a CD containing the list of Fredericksburg voters, compiled by and available from the Virginia State Board of Elections. The chair's messenger was told that the volunteer did not have any such CD or printout of the voters' list but that the chair, as the head of the FDC, should already have it and, if not, should know where to obtain it. Two weeks before the election, the chair of the FDC didn't even have the current voters' list and didn't seem to know whom to contact for one.

Meanwhile, the paid Kerry area representative said that the entire city of Fredericksburg would be canvassed by the local university's Democratic student organization. This was a canvass that should have been done many months before, not two weeks prior to the election. There was a total lack of effective strategic planning, coordination, and communication.

Canvassing: Done by the local college Democrats with complete lack of direction. It is almost analogous to the former Coalition Provisional Authority (CPA) in Iraq under L. Paul Bremer, where young twenty somethings were selected to work for the CPA from a pool of resumes submitted to a Republican, conservative institute and who, with no expertise, ended up heading sections of the CPA tasked with spending billions of dollars for reconstruction projects in Iraq. It was hardly a recipe for success and neither was this so called canvass.

Armed with a minimally adequate questionnaire and limited, effective training, these eager but undirected students did the best they could under the circumstances. They didn't even have handouts to give to those whom they would identify as Kerry supporters! They were given an upcoming Democratic rally flyer to distribute during their canvass, but, whether due to miscommunication or choice, failed to do that.

Contrary to what the Kerry representative said, the canvassing did not cover the entire city of Fredericksburg. Many sections were not canvassed at all. The canvassing was done during approximately a few selected days beginning around October 21. It was too little, too late. It was a voter identification canvass that should have been done many months earlier for effective results usage by the campaign and the Democratic Party.

Phone Bank: A local union had donated its facilities. According to the Kerry area representative, the phone bank was supposed to be up and running by October 18. However, the phone bank would only be in operation Monday through Friday, October 18 through October 29, 9:00 a.m. until 8:00 p.m., and no weekends!

A volunteer list was compiled from a hodgepodge of lists and volunteers contacted by email or phone to arrange a tentative schedule.

However, on the first day, four out of the five phones were not working. There seemed to be a complete lack of communication between the Kerry campaign and the union. It took a number of days before the phones were fixed, requiring canceling volunteers' time, for some the only time they were available, reworking schedules, etc.

As with the college students' canvassing, phone bank workers had inadequate direction, inadequate questionnaire completion forms, and poor phone scripts. For example, there was a question about Congressional candidates when no Democratic candidate's name appeared on the ballot in the First Congressional District. Unfortunately, the contact lists that the volunteers were working from were rough voter identification lists not get-out-the-vote (GOTV).

While the Kerry representative distributed sections of the list to the phone bank volunteers, the sources from which the list was compiled remained a mystery. However, many volunteers soon realized that they were contacting mostly Republicans! This was not the GOTV that they had expected. Many felt their efforts were futile with this kind of disorganization. Some left in dismay. Again, like the canvassing, phone bank voter ID should have been done many months before. The last weeks of the campaign and Election Day should have been exclusively devoted to GOTV. Since Democrats and Kerry voters hadn't been identified previously, they couldn't be targeted effectively in a GOTV phone effort.

Compare this to Republican phone banks where volunteers were able to work at home using their own desktop computers and home phones or at the "bank" using their own laptops and cell phones while working from lists on their monitors that had been compiled from a variety of sources including subscription lists from targeted publications.

Officials from the FDC always complained that they were unable to compete with Republican efforts due to lack of money but there had been little, if any, fundraising activities by the FDC. What had they been doing since the 2000 election to fill their treasury? Why was this election such a complete surprise?

Another major problem that would become a critical factor on Election Day that the chairs and officials of the FDC, STDC, and the SPDC did not understand was the importance of precinct captains. None of the officials seemed to know anything about or have any grasp of the basics of political party organization.

Ward leaders, precinct captains, and block captains are the foundation of effective, local political organizing. This is the Democratic Party structure on which the local, state, and national party and their campaigns should rely. It seemed to be a completely foreign concept to the Democratic Party in Fredericksburg, Stafford, and Spotsylvania. No precinct captains existed in every precinct, let alone block captains or ward leaders

Meanwhile, even though there wasn't any organized campaign activity by the FDC, the authors and other Kerry supporters in Fredericksburg were active during October with the following:

Vice Presidential Debate Party: (authors' house) Kerry supporters watched the televised event held at Case Western Reserve University.

Vote for Change Concert Finale Party: (authors' house) Co-sponsored with MoveOnPAC and ACT (America Coming Together), Sundance Channel offered coverage of an extraordinary musical and political event broadcast live from Washington, D.C. with Bruce Springsteen, John Mellencamp, and a host of other performers.

Kerry Mobile: One of the authors turned a Lincoln Town Car into a traveling Kerry campaign advertisement including endorsement stickers from the UAW, IAFF, Iron Workers Union, Veterans and Latino groups, etc. along with flying American flags and a show of support for US military.

IAFF Campaign Sign: A local Democrat and Vietnam veteran displayed a giant 4 foot by 8 foot yellow and black "International Association of Fire Fighters (IAFF) for Kerry" sign, spotlighted at night and topped with American flags, in his front yard on a prominent main street in the area. It became a well known point of interest during the campaign. (One Sunday morning, vandals cut down the sign but it was raised again that same day.)

Meet the Trains: For a week before and through Election Day, a group of local Democrats, not affiliated with the FDC, set up a table near the train station with campaign materials for free distribution and met and greeted commuters and riders on all outgoing morning and incoming afternoon and evening trains.

A Subdivision Canvass: Another member of the above group canvassed his subdivision one weekend to identify Kerry supporters and GOTV.

Local Debate: "Ask Questions of the Republican and Democrat" sponsored by a local church at the main library almost turned into a Republican tour de force until the FDC officials in attendance were rescued by Kerry supporters skilled in debate and campaign tactics.

Newspaper Advertisement: Another group of local Kerry supporters collected donations for a full page ad in the local/regional paper that featured quotes from and names of area residents who were voting for Kerry.

Second Debate Party: Held at a local restaurant with the televised debate preceded by local guest speakers.

Kerry Rally: Held on October 24 at a local park, with food, entertainment, and guest speakers. This was the metamorphosis of an idea suggested and then scheduled by the Kerry area representative. It was pulled together at the last minute by seven Kerry supporters/volunteers.

Unfortunately, it was the wrong rally, at the wrong time, for the wrong audience. This was a rally that should have been held right after the Democratic convention to enlist volunteers in order to utilize them in an ongoing, organized effort. Running around at a rally on October 24 to sign up volunteers for a phone bank that was supposed to be active on October 18, does not indicate an effective strategy in place. This rally, if held in August or September, could have also been used to attract the curious and perhaps undecided voter. It was another example of too little, too late.

Countdown to Election: 3 Days

October 30, 2004

Three days before the election, a special FDC "meeting" was held in the regional Democratic Committees' monthly coffee klatch venue. The primary activity, directed by the chair, consisted of attendees trying to cover with black ink markers "paid for by the Democratic Party" that appeared on campaign materials.

There was a disagreement between the Kerry representative and the FDC chair regarding sample ballots with the representative for and the chair against distribution. Democratic Party sample ballots are a staple of elections in many communities and should have been distributed at least one or two weeks prior to Election Day.

In the midst of all the artistic activity, the following question came from the floor: "Based on the statistics from the 2000 election when voters in the FDC's bailiwick cast a specific number of ballots for Al Gore, how many additional Democratic votes could the FDC project for Kerry in Fredericksburg?" There was stunned silence. No answer, just officials' mouths hanging open.

These are figures that should trip off the tongue and are at the fingertips of Democratic county/committee chairs, even more quickly in the twenty-first century with helpful computer technology. However, three days before an important presidential election and the FDC chair and other officials present stood mute.

An appropriate description of this event and the FDC seemed to be captured by a woman attendee sitting and knitting while repeatedly asking, "Why are we here?" *Alice in Wonderland* meets *Tale of Two Cities* and Madame Lafarge.

Countdown to Election: 1 Day

November 1, 2004

Where was the FDC activity?

Meanwhile, Kerry supporters were conducting various GOTV efforts including "Meet the Trains" at the local commuter station with large campaign signs and targeted phone calls.

Election Countdown—What? Is it really today?

November 2, 2004

FDC activities: It seemed to consist primarily of placing previously hoarded yard signs at polling places, getting a few people to monitor polls and passing out sample ballots, campaign door hangers, and other campaign materials at polling places.

For Fredericksburg voters, in this election, there was really no contested race other than that for president. The First Congressional District, just as in 2002, had no Democratic candidate running against the Republican incumbent. Unlike a local or state election where voters might need a reminder as to who the multiple candidates are, voters already knew who the candidates were in this presidential election. All the yard signs, sample ballots, door hangers, and other campaign materials should have been distributed and utilized long before Election Day.

On Election Day outside each precinct, there were no precinct captains or block captains who knew, were acquainted with, or recognized most of the Democratic voters from their neighborhoods, blocks, subdivisions, and precincts. One precinct had someone with a schedule of workers but no list of Democratic voters.

There were no precinct captains outside every precinct with their list of identified voters for Kerry, marking the names off as the voters arrived or exited. There were no precinct captains who could immediately see the names of those who hadn't voted yet and needed to be contacted via their handy cell phones. There were no precinct captains at the polling places to send runners/chauffeurs to missing voters' houses to remind them and/or bring them to the polls. There was no evidence of even a minimum, basic Democratic Party election organization.

Meanwhile, on Election Day, one of the authors traveled in the Kerry Mobile, throughout the day, among the wards and precincts, in addition to conducting independent GOTV efforts on a personal cell phone outside polling locations and at the local train station.

Traveling to the various precincts in the Kerry Mobile, the author helped relieve volunteers who had no replacements or take the place of non-existent volunteers in some precincts. Lack of planning seemed endemic.

Outside one precinct, at a second visit around noon, the author, who was independently gauging voter turnout, asked an exiting voter what his number had been in the voting line. The answer was 458. The author knew there was big trouble. This was a heavily Democratic, African American precinct and the number should have been at least double for that time of day.

An official of the FDC happened to arrive at that moment and, when told by the author about the tally, looked shocked and began mumbling in disbelief. The FDC official rushed into the polling place only to discover it was true. This incident was a prime example of the reality that there had been no effective voter identification and therefore no effective GOTV campaign. Like the national campaign, this precinct's Democratic voters had been taken for granted, ignored, or forgotten. The FDC had broken one of the cardinal rules of successful political strategy, if they ever knew it to begin with: ***never take any vote for granted.***

Post Election Review

November 3, 2004

The 2004 election was a repeat of the 2000 fiasco, minus the hanging chads, but this time the state was Ohio not Florida. Bush supposedly won the popular and the electoral vote. Amid this national election picture, Kerry won in Fredericksburg by 695 votes. No pats on the back for the FDC, however. This particular area usually goes Democratic no matter what. However, the Democratic ticket should have won by at least 625 additional votes.

Stafford and Spotsylvania counties should have shown a significant increase in the percentage of Democratic votes because of the changing demographics resulting from more people moving into the area from northern Virginia. Instead, the STDC and the SPDC lost their counties by significant margins to the Republican GOTV. The STDC had only 37.4% voting for Kerry and the SPDC had only 36.7%.

The FDC is a microcosm of the state, the region, and a large part of the nation that comprises the South, Midwest, and West, the so called red states. There is no real Democratic Party organization in Fredericksburg. It is just a moribund, local Democratic Party. It seems to be only a social club. There is no real leadership. There is no identified Democratic political base in place.

It has no foundation of block captains, precinct captains, or ward leaders who work on a regular, neighbor to neighbor basis, identifying Democrats, stroking veteran Democrats, and registering new Democrats year around. There is no Democratic welcome wagon. There is no outreach to lifelong, new, and potential Democrats with newsletters, emails, etc., not even during campaigns. There is no concept that creating, maintaining, and increasing a Democratic base requires 24/7/12 work, not just during two, four, and six year election cycles.

There is no ongoing coordination with traditional and new Democratic groups such as unions, grassroots organizations, etc. There are no regular, more-than-once-a-year events sponsored and/or hosted by the FDC that are an integral part of the community scene, and great for public relations. FDC does no regular public relations, marketing, or communication. There are no recurrent fundraising or development projects. There was no web site even in the twenty-first century.

After the 2000 presidential election debacle, there seemed to be no after action analysis since the FDC was certainly not prepared for 2004. There was no strategic planning. There was no advance planning. There was no voter identification. There was no effective GOTV. There were no grassroots efforts. There were no campaign events planned, implemented, or sponsored by the FDC.

Almost all of the campaign activities and events listed on previous pages were planned and implemented by local Kerry grassroots supporters not affiliated with the FDC. In fact, local grassroots activities and work were not planned, led, or conducted by either the FDC or the national Kerry campaign. The Kerry house parties in the tri-county area—an inadequate imitation of the Dean meet-ups and get togethers according to experts—seemed to be a "not-really-grasping-the-grassroots-concept" effort. Too little, too late to be effective, it was almost non-existent in Fredericksburg.

By 2004, grassroots activists and some Democratic candidates' campaigns recognized that many local and district Democratic Committees in Virginia had no solid, political organizing foundation. The committees not only did not have their fingers on the pulse of their Democratic base or potential new Democratic voters, they didn't know how to take a pulse reading, or even find the patient.

Yes, there were some exceptions statewide, but obviously not enough. Organizations are not successful because of exceptions. For all their protestations to the contrary, most local Democratic Party Committees in Virginia seem accustomed to being a permanent minority party, merely satisfied with an occasional win. It's kind of a perpetual Chicago Cubs mentality: wait until next year. But next year is usually a repeat of the previous losing year.

From the local Democratic Party level to the DNC, the presidential campaign was based on an illusion of a well-organized party with a strong base. That was not the reality. A base cannot be tapped let alone enlarged until it is correctly identified, cultivated, and nurtured. It's an ongoing process. It can't be effectively done in just the few months before an election.

The Democratic Party has been sleepwalking. It sat back during the Clinton years, complacent with the status quo, unconcerned with an effectual, continuing change, and a need for grassroots renewal and revitalization. Even the Congressional elections disaster of 1994 didn't seem to be enough of a wake up call.

After their dramatic loss in 1964, the Republican Party radicals began successfully building their base. They and the current right wing neocons (a group of regressive, Republican conservatives, many a part of or with ties to the Bush administration and a dominant publication and media network, who strongly promote a United States corporate and military global empire) did their work well. There have been only two Democratic presidents in those forty years since Lyndon B. Johnson: Jimmy Carter, one term, and Bill Clinton, two terms.

There are more registered Democrats than Republicans in the United States. They didn't all show up at the polls, again. Why not? Maybe, if every local Democratic Party Committee had spent the last four years really working steadily at identifying Democratic voters, registering new voters, energizing its base, reminding them what the Democratic Party stands for, what it does for them, and that being a Democrat was in a voter's own self interest, a Democratic president would have been sitting in the White House in January 2005. Unfortunately, it seems many were like the FDC, part-time dabblers without a clue.

The city of Fredericksburg, Stafford County, and Spotsylvania County are located in the northern part of the First Congressional District. The FDC chair also served as the First Congressional District Committee chairperson. The First Congressional District did not have a Democratic candidate running against the incumbent Republican in this election nor in 2002. The neighboring Sixth and Seventh Districts also had no Congressional Democratic candidates during this election. Thus, three of eleven Congressional districts in Virginia did not even have a Democratic candidate on the ballot as a choice for the voters!

There was an independent candidate who threw his hat in the ring at almost the eleventh hour against the Republican incumbent in the First Congressional District. This independent candidate's campaign consisted of standing outside supermarkets soliciting signatures to get his name on the ballot and when successful, writing a few letters to the editor of the local newspaper. He received 20 percent of the vote without spending much money or expending much effort.

There were complaints from the STDC and the FDC that the Kerry campaign didn't do enough to help in their locales. While that may have been true, why would the campaign expend time and funds in a Congressional district that twice, consecutively, didn't even bother to field a Democratic challenger for the House of Representatives seat? Coattails work both ways. If those three Congressional districts had Democratic candidates running, it would have forced the Republican incumbents and the Republican National Committee (RNC) to spend money they hadn't counted on spending and helped the Kerry ticket by approximately 136,000 votes.

However, present and future Democratic candidates should begin to realize that it was the grassroots that ran the effective, "professional" campaign. It was not the DNC or its Washington insiders with their record of perennial losses. This election saw Democratic losses in the House and Senate races, also. Those so called professional campaign wizards seem only to care about the primaries and working for the winner so they can make millions of dollars. They really don't care who wins an election. After this and other Democratic defeats, they return to their Republican corporate clients who supported Bush and donated millions to his campaign for business as usual.

The Fredericksburg Democratic Committee is a prime example, there are others with varying gradations, of what is wrong with the Democratic Party. It is like an unfruitful tree. Old, dead branches need to be pruned away so that new, seminal shoots can grow, thrive, and reinvigorate the tree.

Only "outside the beltway" activists who are passionate about politics and core Democratic ideals, values, and vision can restore or create a truly organized, strong, basic structural foundation utilizing technological tools. It will take these intelligent, effective, grassroots organizers to transform the current moribund, myopic, lost-its-way entity into the old fashioned, twenty-first century, dynamic, winning, people powered majority party that the Democratic Party should be.

PART III
Bottom Up Election Reform

Fix the Foundation

Here is a picture of the 2004 presidential election in many states: claims of serious voting irregularities and fraud; voter suppression; voter disenfranchisement; intentional reduction of voter participation; increased numbers of voters but decreased numbers of voting machines in heavily Democratic precincts causing long lines, especially in Ohio and Florida (in some places it was officially reported that voters waited more than six hours); election officials, either inadvertently or deliberately, giving voters incorrect information, primarily about provisional ballots; electronic voting machine problems such as not recording the voter's choice correctly on the screen or otherwise malfunctioning; lack of paper trails to verify voters' selections; optical scanners not recording or misreading ballots; more votes than voters in some precincts; official police presence at, and, in some cases, inside polling places; and more complaints, thousands of them.

Four years after the 2000 debacle, another presidential election is clouded by charges of thousands of incidents of serious irregularities and fraud. Millions of voices across the United States are calling for real election reform. It is an issue that should have bipartisan support. Voters believe that they have a right to vote and trust that their votes count. However, what if, currently, in the United States, the principle of one person, one vote is not really true?

During the 2000 election debacle, the Supreme Court, apparently playing a political rather than its judicial role, decided to stop the Florida recount and selected George W. Bush as president. This Supreme Court, on many occasions, has indicated that the Constitution has no specific clause that grants individuals the right to vote.

In addition, as legal scholars point out, in Bush v. Gore, the Supreme Court, in a five to four vote along party lines, emphasized that state legislatures have the power to bypass the popular vote and select presidential electors. It's possible that legislatures in contested states would appoint their own electors and the popular vote would be of no importance or consequence.

It is not lost on Republican operatives that the more disruption caused in the voting process in so called swing states, the greater the chance that, through legal maneuvering, disputed, close elections may end up with Republican majority state legislatures in those swing states selecting the Electoral College electors.

Today a conservative, Republican dominated Supreme Court consistently chips away at the right to vote and seems to prefer the Electoral College rather than the popular vote to decide presidential elections, protestations that the Bush v. Gore decision was a singular occurrence to the contrary. This challenge to the American electorate certainly calls for a constitutional amendment declaring the basic right to vote.

It is also time to abolish the Electoral College. The Electoral College can be unjust and unfair in the way it apportions electors and dismisses the will of the majority of voters. No reform of the voting process on the state or local levels can mean anything if the right to vote is not enshrined in the Constitution or if the Electoral College can ignore and circumvent the popular vote. Voting then becomes nothing but an empty exercise.

Two constitutional issues should be a priority of the Democratic Party:

1) Confirming the right to vote.
2) Repealing the Electoral College

Until constitutional amendments are passed on these issues, Democratic senators should use these two issues as a litmus test for judicial nominees to the federal courts and Supreme Court. If nominees don't believe that the right to vote should be specifically stated in the Constitution and don't believe that the Electoral College should be abolished, they should not receive any Democratic senator's confirmation vote.

Blind Trust in the Current Voting Hodgepodge

Redistricting has traditionally been done after every ten year census. It's a redrawing by states of Congressional district boundaries to better reflect population changes since the last census. Often it is used to influence the outcome of elections. While it should only be based on population changes to determine representation, historically, all political parties have been guilty of playing with state maps to create a majority for their party in as many voting districts as possible and weaken the other parties. The party in control of the state legislature has the power with this issue. However, the Republican Party added a new twist to this process in 2003.

The egregious example was in the state of Texas where the Republican controlled legislature and governor, with the unethical and possibly illegal interference of a U.S. House of Representatives member, Tom DeLay (R-TX), decided to "re-redistrict" the state's Congressional boundaries. These boundaries had already been redrawn after the 2000 census by federal judges after the Republican majority state senate and the Democratic controlled House reached a stalemate on the remapping process. After the Republicans snatched control of the House in 2002, the Republican majority in the Texas legislature threw out the approved map and created one to their advantage.

In an attempt to halt the process, Texas Democratic legislators left the state and went to neighboring Oklahoma and New Mexico, beyond the jurisdiction of the Texas state police. They denied the Republicans a voting quorum and blocked the Republican drawn redistricting plan that was going to cost the Democrats five seats in Congress. Rep. Tom DeLay's office inappropriately, and some say illegally, used agencies of the Department of Homeland Security (for which he was only admonished by the Republican controlled House Ethics Committee) to try and find the Democratic legislators. In the end, the Republicans had their way and gained the additional Congressional seats.

Many Democrats say that perhaps the Illinois state legislature, which has a majority of Democrats, should pull a "Republican Texas re-redistrict," as a tit for tat. It's an issue that deserves closer examination because of this Texas precedent. Every time the majority party of state legislatures changes, another redistricting would be possible and there could be continuous redistricting, thus, perpetual voting upheaval (Which district are we in this year?) rather than the traditional once every ten years.

The 2000 Florida election debacle also exposed the jumbled voting system that exists in the United States today. Lack of a uniform voting process among counties in Florida—like many states, some counties used punch cards, some optical scanners, etc.—was one of the reasons that the Supreme Court decided to halt the vote count in that state.

Because of the 2000 election disaster, in October 2002, Congress passed the Help Americans Vote Act (HAVA) which mandated that all states improve their election procedures including such aspects as voter registration process and voting machines. This was a response to the punch cards and hanging chads problem in Florida.

Implementation was left to the individual states, which automatically guaranteed a wide variety of interpretations that could either help the situation or make it worse. Also, some of the requirements would not take effect until 2006. Therefore, during the 2004 presidential election, many states still had not updated their voters' list and some states still had thousands of deceased persons on their rolls. Many states had not cleared up the problem of double voting, that is, a voter registered in two places; for example, a person who moved from one state to another and was registered in both states.

In addition, Congress earmarked billions of dollars to assist states in fulfilling this mandate. It was a dream coming true for electronic voting machine manufacturers and their lobbyists as states rushed to purchase Evoting equipment. While HAVA did not require touchscreen computer voting machines, most states interpreted the act to mean that there had to be at least one such machine in every voting locality to meet disabled accessibility guidelines.

There has been a long history of voting fraud in this country. Stuffing ballot boxes, dead voters on the rolls who "voted," are classic examples. But, over the years, security procedures have been developed to protect votes. With paper ballots, poll workers open the box to show the first voter that the box is empty. With lever machines, poll workers check the mechanical counters to see that they are set at zero.

What is different now is both the degree and scope of vote fraud. Stuffed ballot boxes or filed mechanisms on lever machines pale in comparison to the possibilities with computer voting equipment. Programmers can create "back doors," a second, undetected entrance, in the software that could be used to change selected numbers of votes simultaneously or sequentially.

Proprietary software can be developed, and may already have been, that contains an almost undetectable "zombie," a dominant code that remains dormant until activated by a trigger which can alter results, making even a hard copy paper trail questionable.

Votes on a regional or national basis can be changed secretly via modems and wireless systems. Electronic voting machines such as DRE's or "Direct Recording Electronic," which are touchscreen computers, increase the possibilities of high tech voting fraud. Poll workers cannot open the machine and inspect the software.

Direct Recording Electronic (DRE) Machines

Facts about most DRE voting machines are these:

1) There is no paper trail. A voter can't be sure that what she or he selected is actually recorded correctly. There can be no recount or audit. Unlike an optical scanner where the paper ballots can be counted to see if they tally with the scanner totals, there is no verifiable audit comparing two independent sources of data, the machine's against a receipt/ballot, which should match.

2) The software is proprietary and manufacturers refuse to allow the code to be examined. In cases where there were clearly fraudulent elections, courts and vendors have refused to allow independent computer experts to examine the software source code because manufacturers expressed an overriding need for secrecy. Proprietary interests trump voters' rights. In addition, the Federal Election Commission provides only voluntary standards, while state and national certification requirements for DRE voting machines are much less stringent than the standards for the security of other computer products. The DRE machines for bridal registry in retail stores have to meet higher security standards than those for voting!

3) Manufacturers simply say "trust us" and states simply say "trust them." However, would anyone use an ATM machine that did not give the customer a transaction receipt? Does the customer trust that no receipt is necessary because neither the bank nor the computer ever makes a mistake? Yet, in the most important transaction process in this country, voting, a voter is told to trust the electronic voting machine to be perfect with no means of verification.

DRE Manufacturers

While there are a number of electronic voting machine companies the primary manufacturers are:

Election Systems & Software (ES&S) is currently the largest. It was founded by two brothers. One brother is still with the company while the other brother is president of the second largest company, Diebold. Interestingly, Senator Chuck Hagel (R-NE), was the CEO of ES&S until he resigned to run for the Senate in 1996. He was the first Republican in 24 years to win a Senate seat from Nebraska. When he ran for his second term in 2002, he won by a landslide. His company built and programmed the machines that recorded and counted the votes in both those elections. In 2002, ES&S electronic voting machines counted 80 percent of the votes cast. The parent company of ES&S, McCarthy & Company, in which Hagel still owned stock in 2003, valued at $1 million to $5 million, is run by Michael McCarthy who, until 2002, served as Hagel's treasurer/campaign finance director.

Diebold is the second largest. Its CEO, Wally O'Dell, a major Bush campaign organizer and donor, is best known for writing a letter to Ohio Republicans promising to "deliver the vote" for George W. Bush. Did he "deliver" Ohio? Election 2004 vote tabulations give him the right to claim that he did, possibly with the help of Ohio Republican Secretary of State Kenneth Blackwell, the Katherine Harris of 2004. (Harris was Florida's Republican Secretary of State in 2000, and like Blackwell in Ohio, head of Bush's state campaign in Florida).

ES&S and Diebold control almost 80 percent of the electronic voting machine tabulation "market."

Triad Governmental Systems, Inc. wrote the program that tabulated the punch card ballots in 41 counties in the disputed Ohio vote count. The founder of this family run company is a generous supporter of the Republican Party and the Bush campaign.

VoteHere is a company whose chairman in 2003, Admiral Bill Owen, was a member of the Defense Policy Board, the Pentagon's advisory group formerly headed by Richard Perle, a leading neocon. Former CIA director, Robert Gates, of Iran-Contra fame, also served on the board.

Hart Intercivic voting machines also do not provide a paper record.

In 2004 only two companies, *Avante* and *Accupoll*, sold touchscreen machines with a paper trail.

Many voting reform supporters are concerned that the American public's voting rights have been hijacked by or sold out to private companies. Many of these companies, the majority owned by Republicans, have made millions selling machines that eliminate any paper voter verification and audit process. Some states that use optical scanners have passed legislation that prevents the public from using the paper ballots to verify the scanning machines results. Yet, an MIT/Cal Tech study concluded that no method worked more reliably than hand-counting paper ballots.

Before and following the 2000 election fiasco, during and after HAVA was passed by Congress, many prominent computer scientists and experts had been sounding the alarm about electronic voting machine problems, both those that had already occurred and those that were potential and probable. One well known computer science professor stated, "Any programmer can write code that displays one thing on the screen, [yet] records something else...."

Hundreds of articles and many books have been written about this subject. There are web sites dedicated to exposing and warning about this problem. There are hundreds of ways to tamper with computer voting systems without apparent detection.

Two examples: 1) a computerized voting machine passes a less than rigorous acceptance test because the vote tampering software has been programmed via imbedded time and day trigger not to execute until election day, 2) technical servicing can mean installing an upgrade "patch" which does not go through any official approval and which may have been actually designed to more efficiently tamper with votes. However, even if there were approval of patches, there is no assurance that the upgrade installed was the one officially approved.

Diebold machines were easily "hacked," that is, entering a supposedly secure system without detection. These machines were so insecure that the city council of one large city was advised by a voting machine expert to purchase optical scanners that had a paper trail—voters' ballots, rather than purchasing less than secure Diebold touchscreens which were six times more expensive and without a paper audit trail.

In 2003, Diebold admitted that the source code for their machines, which had been examined without their cooperation by independent computer scientists and found to be extremely flawed and easily hacked into to change voting results, had been used in the 2002 November general elections in Georgia and Maryland.

In Georgia in 2002, computerized voting machines, many without paper trails, claimed that incumbent, Senator Max Cleland, a Democrat and decorated, triple amputee, Vietnam veteran, lost to Saxby Chambliss, who avoided Vietnam service with a student deferment and then a bad knee "medical deferment" and ran a campaign that implied he was more patriotic than Cleland. Cleland had a significant lead in all the polls prior to the election. To this day, many in Georgia say the only reason Cleland lost was because of manipulation of the DRE machines. The Evoting machine results could not be recounted or validated.

In 2003, there were bills introduced in the US House and Senate to require all voting machines to produce a voter verified paper trail. Rep. Rush Holt (D-NJ) introduced legislation, The Voter Confidence and Increased Accessibility Act of 2003 (H.R. 2239), in the US House of Representatives. Two key provisions of that act were:

1. Required all voting systems to produce a voter-verified paper record for use in manual audits and recounts (voters could view and check the accuracy of their votes and election officials could use the paper trail to verify votes in the event of computer malfunction, hacking, or other irregularity).

2. Banned the use of undisclosed software and wireless communications devices in voting systems.

That bill, like a similar Senate bill, was bottled up in committee by regressive, Republican Congressional majority leaders to prevent voting reform legislation from reaching the floor.

Many computer technology experts were stupefied that the Democratic Party wasn't doing anything effective to prevent potential DRE voting problems long BEFORE the election in 2004. Every state's Democratic Party, using computer experts who had sounded the alarm, should have led the movement to ensure that every state's voting system(s) had a voter verifiable paper trail.

Why didn't the state Democratic Parties direct their Congressional District Democratic Committees and other local committees to mount a campaign encouraging Democratic and independent voters (and Republican voters, since this was clearly a bi-partisan issue) to contact via email, phone and/or postal mail their Congressional representatives to support and pass Rep. Rush Holt's bill? Again, the Democratic Party was behind the curve and it may have cost Democrats another presidential election.

Among the Democratic presidential candidates, it seems only Howard Dean and Dennis Kucinich thought this issue was important enough to write major articles warning the American electorate about it.

Fixing the Machine Problem

In addressing the machine problem, another issue needs to be mentioned. Since a presidential election is conducted nationwide, many voting reform advocates believe that there should be a uniform standard for national elections.

The following are just a few examples of lack of uniformity:

- Some states have "no excuse required" absentee balloting while others, like Virginia, require a reason for requesting an absentee ballot.

- Some states have same day voter registration, that is, the voter may register on Election Day; others have specific date deadlines prior to an election.

- Some states allow ex-felons to vote; others, like Florida, do not.

- Some states have early voting when citizens can cast ballots at designated places up to 21 days before Election Day; other states have only one day for casting ballots in person.

Of course, the lack of uniformity in methods of voting occurs not just among the states but also intrastate—different localities have different voting methods, some use optical scanners, some DRE's, etc.

A uniform standard for national elections deserves serious consideration and discussion in light of two consecutive presidential elections clouded by claims of fraud, voter suppression and disenfranchisement, and questionable procedures and processes.

Tom Stoppard, the playwright, once said, "It's not the voting that's democracy, it's the counting." The infamous Joseph Stalin stated, "Those who cast the votes decide nothing. Those who count the votes decide everything." Their remarks certainly ring true since electronic voting machines entered the picture, almost monopolized by the two largest, Republican owned companies, ES&S and Diebold.

Many electronic voting machine supporters point to the following benefits of computer voting: 1) meets the needs of disabled voters, 2) solves such problems as over voting and voter intention, 3) can handle multi-lingual requirements. However, work on developing more secure machines is still ongoing. In addition, current electronic voting machines almost require that every polling place have at least two officials, one from each party, who are not just computer literate but computer experts. Although, given the incidents during the 2004 election, even that doesn't guarantee every machine or software problem at the polling site can be fixed. Nonetheless, these computer voting machine advocates agree that all DRE's can and must produce voter verifiable paper receipts/ballots.

These machines, used nationwide in 2004, as well as in prior elections, were capable of producing paper receipts. Manufacturers seemed to have bamboozled purchasing states by claiming excessive extra costs to add this feature, which was completely untrue. Diebold manufactures ATM machines which produce paper receipts for customers, yet, according to Diebold's top managers, their voting machines couldn't produce receipts for voters without an additional, exorbitant cost. They insist that voters don't need a verifiable receipt for confirmation or an audit trail for poll officials. Just trust them.

Recently, conveniently after the presidential election, Diebold officials stated that their DRE machines will now be able to miraculously supply paper receipts.

Voting machines and their codes should be open and transparent, not proprietary, that is, secret. The public and their representatives in government should have the legal right to look at the source code. If a ballot box can be opened before voting begins to show that it is empty and lever machines can be opened to check that their mechanisms are set at zero, then electronic voting machine source code must be open to examination and verification. Proprietary claims by partisan, Republican dominated companies regarding voting machines are disingenuous and should not be supported by the courts.

In addition to a voter verifiable paper audit receipt, another solution is "open source" software for all voting machines. This is a software program whose creators agree to release and make available to the public the source code from which they wrote the program. Since the public has a right to examine the source code, any glitches, security problems, other flaws, or potential to tamper with an election would be exposed. Every company would have a right to the software, so if one company is unreliable or unsatisfactory, the purchasing state and/or locality could use another company with little or no disruption or cost.

Many voting reform advocates believe that Congress, in passing HAVA, and the states, in a rush to implement the mandate by purchasing DRE's with no voter verifiable paper trail or audit record, may have ignored or been unaware of an interesting and surprising voting study. A few years ago Caltech and MIT conducted a research project. It compared the reliability of voting systems used nationwide between 1988 and 2000. Their findings were startling. Hand counted paper ballots were discovered to be the most accurate of voting methods, "better than anything else." *The two worst methods were touchscreen systems (DRE) and punch cards.*

In the rush to pass and implement HAVA, Congress and the states missed the simplest and fairest solution for upgrading the voting process: voting by mail, which is the system successfully used in the state of Oregon.

In every state, a ballot would be mailed to each registered voter's address, where it would be completed by the voter, with a signature verification, and returned. There would be provisions for voters who failed to receive their mailed ballot by a certain date. Returned ballots would be read by optical scanners, checked and certified by state and party officials and independent computer experts. The entire process would be done by state election workers in the presence of monitors from political parties. There would be a paper trail, the ballots, for comparison with scanner tallies and/or recount.

There would be no need for poll workers, since there wouldn't be any polling places. There would be no long lines because of insufficient numbers of machines, since there wouldn't be any machines. It would meet the needs of voters with disabilities since it would arrive in the mail, be filled out at home, and returned by mail. There would be no need for absentee ballots, except for those voters temporarily out of town, and votes could be cast early, right after the debates, or sent in by the national Election Day deadline. It also would not require a proposed national holiday status for Election Day.

Since this is not a constitutional issue, but a process like filing income tax, it could be implemented, with standards or guidelines, by an act of Congress or by each state legislature.

While the majority of postal workers are people of the highest integrity and dedication, the 2004 election provided a cautionary tale to voting by mail. Shortly after the election, one of the authors stopped and talked to a postal carrier who had a Bush-Cheney campaign sticker on the postal vehicle. When reminded that it was not appropriate and might be a violation, the postal carrier simply shrugged a shoulder and said, "So what, the election's over." There have been incidents throughout the nation during the past twenty years or more of postal carriers discarding entire sacks of mail in dumpsters. How many ballots, those mailed to voters or completed returns, on this particular postal carrier's route, might not have reached their destination, if mailed ballots were the voting process in this state?

The Democratic Party at state levels and Democratic Party committees on local levels should lead the movement to secure election reform. At the very least, the Democratic Party in each state should be in the vanguard of ensuring, through introduction and support of state legislation before 2006, that all electronic voting machines in its state produce a voter verifiable paper trail. The Democratic National Committee should launch a nationwide campaign that brings to the floor of Congress, before the Congressional and gubernatorial elections of 2006, Senate and House bills, such as the bill introduced by Rep. Rush Holt in 2003, which would require voter verified paper receipts on all electronic voting machines.

One Democratic activist indicated that if the Democratic leadership ignores voting concerns and fails to seize and successfully lead the election reform issue, then thousands of grassroots activists—those who raised millions of dollars from average citizens, registered new voters, made the phone calls, did the door-to-door canvassing, and other boots on the ground efforts—might not do it again in 2006 or 2008. The Democratic Party should have been concerned about this problem long before the 2004 presidential election. If the Democratic Party doesn't become effectively involved now, the elections of 2006 and 2008 may be repeats of 2000, 2002, and 2004.

PART IV
Evaluate, Innovate, Reinvent to Win Elections

Evaluating Existing
Resources and Practices

In order to reinvigorate the Democratic Party, officials of city, county, and state committees and their membership, need to evaluate whether they currently have an effective Democratic organization. Through an honest evaluation of existing resources and practices, these state and local organizations should be able to see how and what they need to change.

Growing a grassroots organization begins from the ground up, not the top down. Many city, county, and state Democratic Parties failed in 2000, 2002, and 2004, and some have been moribund for more than twenty-five years.

While experience counts, the experience of inept, indifferent people, satisfied with the status quo, or agreeing only to limited alteration that really doesn't make significant changes in the status quo or their position, means nothing other than an example of what not to do, and should not be acceptable in the Democratic Party. Many of these individuals are currently officials of city, county, state, and national Democratic Party Committees.

"Thank you for your service but for the good of the Democratic Party we must ask you to resign from your office. Instead, we would like you to…" are lines not heard often enough in the Democratic Party. Yes, everyone is valuable but many current Democratic Party officials need to step aside and help in other, more appropriate, ways. New, activist, energized, capable, dedicated Democrats need to be elected to Democratic Party Committee positions.

Across the United States members of Democratic Party Committees should conduct a critical evaluation of existing resources and practices. Some questions that should be asked of every city, county, state, and national Democratic Committee are:

- Is it composed of the best and the brightest, dedicated, activist Democrats?

- Does it convene regular, frequent meetings to increase participation?

- Does it keep everyone, including the media, informed through websites, emails, newsletters, events, etc.?

- Is it always working on creating an inclusive, expanding pool of activist Democrats, from every walk of life, from high school students to senior citizens (voters' lists, campaign volunteers lists, etc. should be a source)?

- Has it trained active block captains, precinct captains, and other Democratic Party leaders including potential replacements and assistants?

- Do current canvassing results include individuals' email addresses?

- Does it have Democratic candidates on the ballot for every elected office?

- Does it sponsor regular events, including fundraisers?

If your committee failed this simple evaluation, it's time to go to work.

Getting the Local Democratic Party Working Again

Many Democratic state and local parties were upset when organizations like America Coming Together (ACT) came into their localities to register and canvass voters, and to do other essential election and campaign work. These groups were doing it because many state and local parties were not.

The Fredericksburg Democratic Committee in the micro study example was the reality of much of the Democratic Party nationwide. There was no effective, strategic plan to reinvigorate the Democratic Party at every level, especially local and state. After the 2000 debacle, 2002 and 2004 seemed a blur of continuing Democratic Party unpreparedness. It was entrenched status quo all the way.

The formal Democratic Party had become, to quote Howard Dean, "Republican-lite" and forgot it was the party of Roosevelt, Truman, and Kennedy. It not only forgot its base, working people in every state and community, it forgot or discarded the basics of Democratic Party organizing. However, over the last thirty years the Republican Party has successfully borrowed traditional Democratic Party tactics that the formal Democratic Party hierarchy had mistakenly thrown away as too liberal and populist. It's time to reclaim them.

Unless the Democratic Party wants to remain the permanent minority party in Congress and continue to lose presidential elections, it must get back to basics. Its ideas, infrastructure, and operation must work from the grassroots up, not from Washington insiders down, while incorporating computer technology and the Internet network, or netroots, as an integral, indispensable component in its revitalization.

Activist Democratic Party members are working hard to change the status quo. If they are thwarted in their efforts by unwilling, resistant party officials, they should use their skills to make noise, make a fuss, create a commotion, and marginalize the cheerleaders and guardians of the failed status quo.

While addressing the two constitutional election reform issues: enshrining the right to vote and abolishing the Electoral College, and, on the process side, assuring voting equality and uniformity in national elections and fixing the electronic voting machine problem, the Democratic Party must return to its organizing basics.

Getting to Know You

Whether election reform results in eventual, nationwide uniform voting by mail, or states continue to use other methods such as electronic voting machines with open source code and paper trails, whatever voting processes have been voter verified as equal and trustworthy, Democratic Party organizing can still use a geographic precinct method for local, grassroots organizing.

Voting precincts nationwide usually consist of some or all of the following, depending on location, whether city, suburban, exurban, or rural: city neighborhoods and streets made up of houses, small businesses such as retail stores, condominiums, apartment buildings; housing subdivisions (just houses or houses, condos, apartments, trailer homes, or various combinations); college or university dormitories; housing in rural areas.

Divide voting precincts into workable areas which, for simplicity's sake, will be called "blocks." Each of these divided areas or blocks has a block captain who is in charge of that block, depending on division size. For example, it might consist of five square city blocks with houses; one large apartment building; one small subdivision; part of a large subdivision; five mile square rural or exurban area; a college dormitory; etc. The entire precinct is divided into manageable parts.

Every precinct has a precinct captain. This captain works closely with the all the block captains in the precinct and reports to and works closely with the local Democratic Committee. In larger communities and cities where multiple precincts constitute a ward, there can also be a ward captain who coordinates precinct captains and works closely with the Democratic Committee.

This approach should be regarded as a traditional, back to the future process, which many Democratic activist great-grandparents and grandparents may recognize. Their Democratic children, grandchildren, and great-grandchildren should understand the concept and easily adapt to this approach because of its social contact and integrated technology.

Block Captains: Backbone of the Democratic Party

Block captains are activist members of the Democratic Party who get to know everyone in their block (size and type varies). It's a neighbor-to-neighbor operation. The first goal is to identify every Democrat, independent, and Republican and gather information, informally educate in a social atmosphere, and offer assistance when necessary. It's the framework that creates the opportunity to do the identification that wasn't effectively done in every precinct around the country for many years. This should be a Democratic Party that doesn't wait until just before the next election to rush around and fail, but is always prepared and successful. It collects baseline information that can be easily and regularly updated.

Block captains personally contact *everyone* in their block and conduct follow-ups on a regular basis throughout the year. The first vital assignment is to take a neighborhood survey, as friendly neighbors; for example, "By the way, who did you vote for in the last presidential election?"

Block captains should be trained to do canvassing to identify the Democratic base, expand that base, educate that base, energize that base, coordinate that base, and most importantly, find out about its concerns. This initial baseline canvassing should be done as soon as possible before 2006 and should only take a few weeks to complete.

This important canvass needs to produce the following information: resident's name, address, phone number, email address, number of voters in household (names, etc.), whether they have ever volunteered and/or did campaign work. These indispensable block captains have canvassed their area and completed vital voter identification, become familiar with the voters in their block, especially Democrats, and laid the groundwork to regularly interact with them.

Block captains keep track of who moves out or moves into the block, a Democratic welcome wagon, and therefore can remind and/or help these Democratic arrivals to register to vote in the state or change their address in state or locally to meet voting deadlines. The block captain will also be able to ascertain, with training, when and how to identify and tap potential, activist Democrats and block captain successors and/or assistants in their block.

Block captains should also host or facilitate Democratic meet-ups/house parties in their blocks so that Democrats can meet and interact with other Democrats. These get togethers should occur regularly during every year not just election years. These meetings could be the vehicle to discuss local, state, and/or national issues; distribute information and materials; plan an en masse contact (via email, phone, and postal mail) of state legislators, Congressional representatives, federal or state agencies, etc. about a particular matter; read and discuss liberal books; plan a local Democratic event with other precincts in the area; become venues for local and state Democratic officials to speak with their Democratic constituents. The possibilities for using this type of gathering to advance and strengthen the Democratic Party are endless.

Precinct Captains

Precinct captains are management level Democratic Party activists with the ability to completely familiarize themselves with the entire precinct, all the blocks or areas. Precinct captains should have the overview of the precinct, the big picture—how many registered Democratic voters, how to increase those numbers, who are or may be the activist Democrats. In addition, they also regularly communicate with media and business people in the precinct.

The precinct captains' main duty is to coordinate their block captains' efforts. They make sure block captains have all the information and materials they need to do their work. They meet regularly with block captains, either separately, in groups, or all together to share information and strategy that will make everyone's efforts more effective.

Precinct captains make themselves available to directly assist block captains for canvassing and other projects, when necessary. They evaluate block captains, which ones are the most effective and which ones might need more training or assistance.

Precinct captains serve as the main conduit between block captains and the local Democratic Committee. This does not mean that block captains should not interact with the local committee, but it's more efficient when they work with and through the precinct captains. Every precinct captain can then give the local Democratic Committee the total picture of the city and/or county of which every precinct is an integral part.

They coordinate what the block captains are trying to accomplish with the goals of the Democratic Committee so that everyone is singing from the same page. While block captains are directly in contact with residents in their block, precinct captains should, over time, become familiar with many of the residents and businesses throughout the precinct.

In very large cities with hundreds of precincts, a certain number of precincts make up a ward. What the precinct captain is to precinct, block, or area organizing, the ward leader is to precinct and precinct organizing. The ward leader is also the coordinator between the ward's precincts and the local Democratic Committee.

Working the Foundation

The methodology of block captains, precinct captains, and ward captains is the basic foundation of the Democratic Party. It is the Democratic Party's visible presence in every neighborhood in every community. When Democratic citizens hold office, this direct contact neighborhood network can tell the Democratic Party officeholders of expressed concerns, things that need to be done such as improving garbage collection, fixing potholes on certain streets, etc. long before they become festering problems. This system enables citizens and their elected Democratic Party officials to have better communications and a closer relationship that does not always require citizens' attendance at formal, local government meetings to have their voices heard. The Democratic Party is the visible "can do" party, the average citizen's party in the community,and when it can't do something, every constituent has been told exactly why and what must be done to change the negative to a positive. The Democratic Party is trustworthy and transparent.

So, what are the qualifications for block, precinct, and ward captains? They must be registered, activist, or willing to be activist, dedicated Democrats who are intelligent, sociable, people oriented, and detail oriented. In addition, precinct and ward captains must have management abilities. How does the Democratic Party find individuals with these qualifications? Some are already known: those who really did the actual work during the Kerry campaign whether Kerry volunteers, MoveOn members, ACT members, Democracy for America members, and others. Many wore multiple hats.

There is an important caveat for all Democratic Party Committees. Block captains, precinct captains, ward captains, and Democratic Party Committee members should all be volunteers or, if one group is paid for work, all should be paid.

During the Kerry campaign, many Kerry representatives who were paid did not really do the grassroots work but, in many cases, took the credit for the work of unpaid volunteers who were unaware of the payment disparity. Fairness should always be the Democratic Party and every Democratic candidate's campaign credo.

Growing the Database

In 2003 and 2004, Democratic primary challengers, and then John Kerry's campaign, along with the DNC, the DCCC, the state and local committees, and other Democratic organizations, large and small, went about the work of gathering some type of information about volunteers, contributors, and the voters they were trying to reach. That information should have ended up in a database for use in future elections and accessible for use in rebuilding the Democratic Party's base. In many cases it did not.

Some candidates and committees hold tight to critical data and information as if it belongs only to them. They do not contribute to a central repository for qualified use by the Democratic Party. Each separate entity keeps reinventing the information wheel ad infinitum.

One major flaw in the Kerry campaign was the central website which did not allow volunteers the option of having email contact information available to access other volunteers. Unlike Howard Dean's grassroots base Internet interaction, Kerry volunteers were unable to easily identify, connect, and communicate among themselves. Communication was controlled top down by Kerry campaign officials. It was a system that frustrated experienced grassroots volunteers and hindered their effectiveness.

Well-structured databases are changing the way elections are targeted from messages to get-out-the-vote efforts. In 2005 and beyond, databases will play an increasingly central role in the business of winning elections. The following list points to a few of the advantages and difficulties the Democratic Party faces managing databases and technology.

1. *Getting quality data and analysis*: Good data doesn't ensure good results by itself, but bad data always yields bad results. It is important to define which data sets are most important and eliminate redundancy and poor information from being included. For example, block and precinct captains need to

regularly review their area's information and provide the local repository with updates that then are forwarded to the central databank.

2. *Using standardized software and applications*: Getting the entire Democratic Party using the same software and uniting behind a well structured, web-based, open source solution should be a priority. That means selecting one extensible software solution from the variety currently being used. Database consolidation by the DNC is a must to become competitive in the twenty-first century.

3. *Maximize the use of unstructured data*: Today's environment of instant media and blogs increasingly relies on and uses a variety of unstructured or semi-structured data. Qualified professionals are pioneering the confluence of information and using good, open source, content management programs to disseminate their results. Improvements are being made every day in using items like emails and document forwarding to provide quick analysis and information for everyone from candidates to campaign workers.

4. *Make quick access available*: While some candidate and party websites existed in prior elections, in 2004's election cycle it became mandatory. The future looks bright for those candidates and parties that "win via the web." From the ability to quickly handle large numbers of small donations to communications, the web is growing in importance.

5. *Expanding the database*: Traditional operational and transactional data still come from the grassroots up, and will continue to do so. Having that data will expand the ability of the Democratic Party to get its message out. In 2004, the Kerry campaign used its database to effectively make tens of thousands of contacts that would not have happened without the dynamism of today's technology.

6. *Canvassing to create/update a database*: Direct canvassing designed to solicit baseline, database information is the responsibility of the local organizations. Once block captains, precinct captains, and their assistants have done a complete direct canvass of every resident in the city and/or county, and every Democratic, Republican and independent voter has been identified, the data they have gathered is then fed into an appropriate database. That database is then compiled and collated against the most recent voters' list by local com-

puter experts. This database is regularly updated with information from block and precinct captains and is therefore always current.

7. *During an election*: Block captains, who know the people in their area, can go directly to Democratic and other targeted voters and do everything possible, from reminders to providing transportation, to get these voters to the polls. Block captains will easily be able to make sure that those who needed absentee ballots received them and that completed ballots are sent or delivered to the registrar on time. If their state now has a voting-by-mail process, they can make sure that every Democratic voter in their block has voted. This is a continuing, organizing operation with direct, personal contact. The system is in place and targeted surveys, issue, primary, and candidate polling, etc. can be done without constantly reinventing the wheel.

Communicating the Message

City, county, and state Democratic Parties should ensure that they, their precinct captains, block captains, and volunteers who work with them, communicate the Democratic Party message, for example, economic fairness, equality, Social Security, etc., in the most effective way, using creative materials and methods. How do they achieve this?

Local Democratic Parties should work co-operatively and in a coordinated manner with progressive organizations such as the Center for American Progress, Rockridge Institute, Economic Policy Institute, and others in order to reach as many area Democrats and other citizens with ongoing, important information that impacts their daily lives. The Democratic message trumps the Republican message, but it must be repetitive and reach the voters. That is every local Democratic Committee's responsibility.

Every local Democratic Committee should have a web site, preferably well designed and user friendly, and a blog. The appropriate use of email addresses that were compiled from the canvassing and regularly updated is a growing tool of every effective organization and an invaluable communication resource.

How important is the use of email in politics? During the presidential election, the Kerry campaign compiled a list of over two million email addresses, but the Republicans had a list of over six million email addresses, a 200 percent advantage.

Those email addresses should receive regular messages from the county Democratic Party about what's happening locally, in the state, and in the nation that is important to the average citizen. The local Democratic Committee web site should interface with Democratic state and national sites and blogs, so that everyone has the same information almost immediately.

The Democratic Party on the local, state, and national level must reach out to their Democratic base via the Internet, not make the base have to search for the Democratic Party.

Every local Democratic Committee also should have other methods, like a newsletter, to communicate with those who don't use computers in their daily lives.

Here is what every city and county Democratic Committee can accomplish with an email and non-computer information network: it can change the Democratic Party from the minority to the majority party again. Right now, it can change policies by being a vocal opposition party. While it may not be able to stop the Bush administration nor Republican controlled local and/or state government from doing counterproductive or harmful things, it can bring this to the voters' attention. It can promote Democratic policies and candidates using this network of block and precinct captains, emails, newsletters, house gatherings, town meetings, etc.

For instance, this Democratic Party network could respond immediately and inundate senators and Congressional representatives, the White House, federal agencies, state, and local governments with emails, phone calls, and postal mail to protest Republican policies or actions. It works. The Republicans and their minions stole it from the Democratic Party and have used it effectively.

State Democratic Parties

The role of the Democratic Party at the state level is fundamental. Since it is composed of members from every city and county party committee in the state, it needs to be aware of what is happening everywhere at the local level. It must coordinate the county and city committees so that there is effective sharing of information and results, what works and what doesn't, among all local committees.

The State Democratic Party must assist the local committees whenever necessary. Some need more help than others. The state Democratic committee must learn from the grassroots local committees because, through their block captains, they know what is really happening on the ground with the Democratic base in their localities—particularly the base's concerns. That occurs from the bottom up not the top down. Those days should be past when the only effective ideas were thought to come from the top down and local Democratic Party officials and members were only followers, not leaders.

However, especially now, when the Democratic Party needs to be re-energized and reinvigorated, there are many entrenched officials at the local level who want to retain their ineffective status quo positions by doing nothing, only making cosmetic changes to their committee, and keeping new, activist Democrats out. Most state Democratic committees know who these individuals and/or groups are and need to use the mechanisms of their charters to make sure they shape up or resign their offices.

The state committee needs to pay attention to new, activist Democrats who make legitimate complaints about current, recalcitrant local and state Democratic Party officials, and quickly and successfully resolve the situation. If not, these activist Democrats, the future of a revitalized Democratic party, will leave in frustration and disgust and the Democratic Party will be the loser.

Coordination and effective communication are the two most important responsibilities of the state Democratic Party committee in its relationship with every local committee and, therefore, among Congressional districts. While local and state committees can tap numerous resources, such as other liberal organizations, to help them do their work successfully, the state committee should also be another resource for local committees.

Every local committee's data base should interface with the state committee's. It must be a strong, interwoven coordination and communication network, working in both directions, vertically as well as horizontally among the various local committees, especially those that compose each state Congressional district.

If every local committee's block/precinct/ward system is working effectively and its communication efforts are top notch, then the coordination among those county and city Democratic committees that constitute a Congressional district should be a "no brainer," that is, it should flow smoothly and effectually. It should be just another interconnection in the Democratic network, with specific goals that are germane to Congressional districts, primarily, the election of a Democratic Congressional representative. The system works for every level of the Democratic Party: local, county, state, and national.

The state Democratic Committee channels the information, background, and other vital communication from the local committees to the Democratic National Committee. The unvarnished picture must be given so that the DNC has a complete nationwide description of the political realities. If every Democratic Party block/precinct/ward system and communication network is working efficiently and effectively in every locality in every state, then there is a strong, national, Democratic organization and network built on a strong, always expanding, local, grassroots foundation. It's an equally winning situation in all fifty states.

Using this methodology as a model can ensure the Democratic Party's return as the nation's majority party, the old fashioned, twenty-first century Democratic Party—the party of working people, current workers, future workers, and past workers. The Democratic Party should be known as the party of the people who work hard and play by the rules.

Turnaround Faces DNC

Any careful evaluation of the current Democratic National Committee would conclude that it is an organization in need of a turnaround. Presidential election losses in 2000 and 2004, the continuing loss of seats in the U.S. Senate and House, declining influence in state after state, and a leadership out of touch with its base, are cold realities that need to be confronted.

While some turnarounds consist of only making minor organizational changes, in the DNC's case, a major overhaul is called for. To do that, it is necessary to realistically evaluate current personnel and practices and develop a strategic plan that incorporates rebuilding from the grassroots up with a national vision.

By 2006, the effectiveness of any turnaround plan should begin to be evident. If the DNC and the DCCC have Democrats running in all 435 House races and evaluate how they performed in races for seats now being held by Republicans, it should provide meaningful data on how well the implementation of the turnaround plan is being accomplished. The following provides a simple timeline for the turnaround:

Evaluation	Transition	Execution	Mid Terms	Future
3 months	6 months	6–10 months	Nov 06	07–08

One immediate item should be a set of "guiding principles" for the DNC, such as: Democratic Party Core Values; People and Volunteers Come First; Create a New Work Culture; Measure Results Incrementally; Obtain Real, Honest Feedback; Work Towards Improving Long-Term People-2-People Relationships.

Modern, Simpler, and Better

Reinventing the Democratic Party throughout the United States may be the most important challenge facing that organization today. From its current minority position, Democrats must pull together behind the newly constituted DNC. Every person in the organization, locally, statewide, and nationally, should be evaluated and every process needs to be analyzed and re-engineered to maximize effectiveness.

For example, three critical areas designed for internal and external communications need to be restructured. The national organization itself needs 1) an intranet, 2) an extranet, and 3) sites for the worldwide web. Consider the DNC's public website. Ask the simple question: Is the DNC even worldwide web ready? Visit the current site at http://www.democrats.org and keep in mind that reportedly in 2004, over 200 million non-English speakers and 150 million English speakers visited political sites.

To most people the site appears cluttered and needs a full makeover.

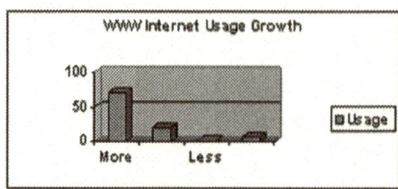

Today's web sites must come alive with graphics that involve people and load fast. Functional sites need to be linked and optional animation graphics, plug-ins, and video need to be handled separately.

Given its audience, the DNC's main public site should use only professional looking graphics and themes. It should become the unifying lodestar for Democratic messages, reports, press releases, newsletters, emails, door tags, bumper stickers, yard signs, banners, etc. The Democratic Senate Campaign Committee, Democratic Congressional Campaign Committee, state and local committees, and other allied web sites should take their cues from it.

What also faces the redesign of a twenty-first century Democratic Party are four very different kinds of voters:

1. Those with no web awareness.

2. Those with limited web awareness.

3. Niche web users.

4. Veteran web surfers.

Interactive sites need to be developed with security, privacy, and process levels in mind. For example:

Level 1—Initial user
Level 2—Committed Democrat (vote, contribution)
Level 3—Involved Democrat (block captain, precinct captain, etc.)
Level 4—Local leadership
Level 5—State/Federal leadership

By the time every level of user is considered, any array of options should include the following:

• Democratic branded email address with an auto forward option

• Searchable directory of members with access determined by member and level of security clearance

• Ability to control member information

• Bulletin boards

- Hosted blog site

- Customizable web portal with local, regional, national, and international news

- Candidate sites

- Job posting

- Online contribution and registration

- Online collaboration

- Content distribution

These options alone will modernize, simplify, and expand participation and inclusion at every level.

PART V
Real Democrats

12 Core Values of a Democrat

Belief in the Constitution and its Bill of Rights as a
Living Document of Inclusion not Exclusion

Life, Liberty and the Pursuit of Happiness for All

Fairness and Equal Opportunity for All

Protection of the Environment

Quality Public Education

Economic Justice for All

Living Wage Jobs

Social Security

Fiscal Responsibility

Workers' Representation and Collective Bargaining

Affordable Health Care, Housing, Utilities and Food

Homeland Security and Strong National Defense

A Democratic Party with Spine

Democrats need to realize that Republicans are currently dictating the rules, and evidence mounts that the Republican Party is attempting to institutionalize a one party system, the Republican Party. Does anyone need to be reminded that Republicans currently control all three branches of our federal government? The legislative, executive, and judicial branches work from the same coordinated "song sheet" along with their think tanks, fundraisers, lobbyists, corporate, and media claques.

During 2004, the Kerry campaign, the DNC, and the various other Democratic campaigns and organizations often acted as if they were separate, independent contractors and failed to deliver a cohesive message. Meanwhile, Republicans offered a coordinated "take no prisoners" attack by Bush, the RNC, and the other Republican campaigns and organizations that created negative impressions of Kerry and the Democratic Party with the voters.

Regressive Republicans are not finished yet. They will continue to do everything and anything they can to gain more power. Going negative is the regressive Republican way. Some insiders report regressive Republicans set campaign media spending at a 10:1 ratio in terms of negative over positive advertising. It worked.

Let's consider one recent example of the results of one party rule. Republican Speaker of the United States House of Representatives, J. Dennis Hastert (R-IL), has proclaimed that the Republican controlled House will consider bills only if "the majority of the majority" supports them.

Given the stated desire of regressive Republicans to amass complete power, pay off their millionaire contributors and special interest groups, especially corporate cronies, while enriching themselves, Democrats are confronted with three choices: surrender to Republican control; make deals and accept the scraps; fight them and go directly to the voters.

Democrats must get tougher by fighting back together. They must learn to fight fire with fire.

Being Pro Active

Run Candidates: County/city/state Democratic Committees must make sure that a Democratic candidate runs for every seat, in every election, locally, state wide, and in every Congressional district—whether dog catcher, school board member, mayor, governor, Congressional representative, whatever—*for every elected office.*

Fundraising: Every local Democratic Committee needs to schedule fundraising events throughout the year; one each quarter is optimum. It can't do its job or help candidates without adequate money in the treasury. Some of these scheduled events, like a picnic or barbecue, should become annual, traditional occasions on the community calendar. If anything was learned from the 2004 election, it was that the ten to fifty dollar contributions of average Democrats added up to millions and acted as a counterbalance to fat cat, corporate money.

Target the Media: If the local newspaper is an unfair and unbalanced Republican rag sheet, the local and state Democratic Party should support those who start an alternative Democratic owned newspaper. If the local radio stations are conservative providers of mostly Limbaugh/Reilly/Hannity and that ilk, and owned by other conservative media or local newspapers, the Democratic Party should consider supporting Democrats who want to restore local control, public value, and another voice, liberal and populist, in the area. Democrats with a few extra coins could purchase and make operational, for as little as $6,000, low power FM (LPFM), non-profit radio stations. While the range is limited, approximately three to four miles, the potential is enormous with a string of these throughout a locality.

Support Other Like Minded Organizations: Members of the Democratic Party, especially those with deep pockets, on the local, state, and national levels should support progressive think tanks like the Center for American Progress, the Rockridge Institute, and the movement to help these and other institutions assist the Democratic Party in becoming a majority party again.

Work with Labor: The Democratic Party's traditional alliance with labor unions, the backbone of the working people who are the backbone of the Democratic Party, should be strengthened on the local and state levels. The Democratic Party should never forget that because of its traditional support of labor unions and labor issues all workers, union and non-union, benefit from the 40 hour work week, overtime pay, workplace protection regulation, child labor laws, and more. It wasn't always that way and attempts are being made by regressive Republicans to revoke these hard won rights.

Guard Our Advances and Continue Making Progress: Together with labor unions and other liberal organizations like Democracy For America, in addition to liberal web sites and blogs such as The Daily Kos, Atrios, The Left Coaster, as well as progressive publications like The Nation, The Progressive, Mother Jones, and others who guard our democratic freedoms, local and state Democratic Parties can build a strong organization and network. All these organizations can help to keep the Democratic Party on track, going in the right direction, and showing the way when it happens to get sidetracked or lost.

Training for the Future: Work with Democratic training organizations like Democracy for America, Latinos for America, Progressive Democrats of America, 21st Century Democrats, Wellstone Action, Progressive Majority, and others to support training as well as motivating current and future grassroots Democratic activists, organizers, and candidates.

All of this has primarily focused on the local county/city Democratic Party Committees because that is the foundation of grassroots organizing, using the block/precinct/ward captain system integrated by ongoing, effective, multi-faceted communication with the local Democratic base, and consolidated by twenty-first century methods such as more creative uses of the Internet.

Get the Facts
About People and Issues

With a corporate dominated media, real facts and news are becoming more difficult to find. Liberal/progressive blogs, web sites, and radio tell it like it is. They are an integral part of Democratic netroots, which is the grassroots on and via the Internet. Listed below are just a very few of these sites and blogs and they will lead the visitor to many other sites and blogs that are also allies, friends, and supporters of the Democratic Party. They give you all the information you need about news and issues that will keep you informed and help you with talking points. Go and visit.

www.democrats.org This is the official site of the Democratic National Committee with links to Democratic office holders, organizations, committees, state sites, etc.

www.democracyforamerica.org Inspired by Howard Dean's presidential campaign, this is a grassroots organization that, among its objectives, identifies and supports fiscally responsible, socially progressive candidates.

www.americanprogress.org This is the site of the Center for American Progress. A feature called *Progress Report* offers news updated daily Monday through Friday.

www.airamericaradio.com This is a 24 hour liberal radio network that is an antidote to the current right wing monopolization of the airwaves.

www.dailykos.com One of the most visited progressive, reform, political blogs.

www.commondreams.org A web site that offers news and views updated daily with a progressive emphasis and vision.

What Can I Do to Help?

Here are some easy things you can do to help elect Democrats. They are listed in order of amount of time and treasure expended. You can do them by yourself or with other Democrats. Remember, whatever contribution you can make is valuable to you, your family and loved ones, your community, your state, and the entire nation.

Vote for Democrats
(Time=minimal   Treasure=priceless)

Make sure that you and everyone you know vote for Democrats! If there is even the slightest possibility that they may not or cannot make it to the polls, *don't take a chance.* Have them complete an absentee ballot application form (available from your local Board of Elections). Instructions and deadlines are usually on the form.

Show the Flag for Democrats
(Time=minimal   Treasure=priceless)

Display yard signs, signs in windows, on doors, and car bumper stickers. Wear Democratic candidates' gear whenever possible: campaign buttons, stickers, caps, lapel pins, etc.

Volunteer for a Local Committee
(Time=depends on you   Treasure=priceless)

Volunteer on the local level and become a sustaining member of the Democratic Party. You could do any number of things from canvassing to becoming a block or precinct captain. Your local Democratic Committee needs your help.

Give Monetary Contributions
(*Time=minimal   Treasure=as much as you can afford*)

Volunteer for a Democratic Candidate's Campaign
(*Time=as much as you can afford for good government*)

Become a Democratic Candidate
(*Time=extensive   Treasure=Priceless*)

True Democratic office holders make a difference that improves peoples' lives in their communities, states, nation, and even the world.

Appendix on the Web

This book is based primarily on the authors' first hand knowledge, experience, and scrutiny. Some elements have been gleaned from the Internet with its World Wide Web, search engines, and blogosphere—an important twenty-first century tool, and an on-line, democratic, open-source method of gathering, sharing, and communicating information.

For example, some of the material about DRE machines and manufacturers was first brought to public attention by voting machine experts and activists including:

Bev Harris http://www.blackboxvoting.org

Lynn Landes http://www.banvotingmachines.org

They were in the vanguard of those alerting voters about the problems with DRE machines and other computer voting methods.

Voter statistics for Virginia may be found on the Commonwealth of Virginia's State Board of Elections site:

http://www.sbe.state.va.us and http://sbe.vipnet.org

For additional information about this book, the authors, archives, current news and views, and author appearances, visit the publisher's web site: http://www.badurina.com

Acknowledgements

Many, many thanks to:

- Roxana Varga for reading the manuscript a number of times and offering invaluable input

- Ron Smith and Mary Beth Smith for providing insightful feedback

- Joseph Edward O'Donnell for his photos of the Kerry rally in Madison, Wisconsin

Special thanks to:

- Dr. Howard Dean, Democratic National Committee Chair, for taking the time to read the pre-publication manuscript and share his thoughts.

True Democrats all!

About the Authors

Drucilla Badurina is president of Badurina & Associates, an advisory firm whose focus has been Croatia and its relations with the United States. She and Badurina & Associates are familiar to many Croatian-Americans and Croatians worldwide. Her articles and interviews have appeared in publications in the United States, Canada, Croatia, Australia, and elsewhere. Drucilla was also the co-founder of a professional ethnic dance company and a performer with that group for a number of years.

A lifelong Democrat, Drucilla has been involved in Democratic politics and campaigns. During this past election, she actively worked as a volunteer for the Kerry-Edwards campaign, primarily with its National Ethnic Outreach, but also with Roman Catholic outreach.

Shawn O'Donnell is a true, "old style," twenty-first century Democrat, and a Virginia First Congressional District businessman. He was the CFO of a software company until he left his job to volunteer for the Kerry-Edwards campaign. Shawn's business and management background and experience span more than three decades and include service, retail, manufacturing, business development, and consulting. His articles about business and economics have appeared in various publications nationally and internationally.

Shawn is a real activist who has managed and worked on Democratic campaigns since the age of 13. His work in the recent presidential campaign as a volunteer for Kerry-Edwards included being active with Information Technology, Media Corps, Catholics for Kerry, and assisting local Virginia Democratic parties.

978-0-595-35620-1
0-595-35620-6